LITHUANIA

NEW & SELECTED POEMS

ALSO BY MYRA SKLAREW

Poetry

In the Basket of the Blind (Cherry Valley Editions 1975)
From the Backyard of the Diaspora (Dryad Press 1976, 1981)
Blessed Art Thou, No-One (Chowder Chapbooks 1982)
The Science of Goodbyes (The University of Georgia Press 1982, 1983)
The Travels of the Itinerant Freda Aharon (Water Mark Press 1985)
Altamira (Washington Writers' Publishing House 1987)
Eating the White Earth (Tag Press 1994)

Fiction

Like a Field Riddled by Ants (Lost Roads Publishers 1988)

Myra Sklarew

LITHUANIA

NEW & SELECTED POEMS

For Edgar Cahn —
With kindest wishes for our beloved May's brother!
Myra Sk

Azul Editions
MCMXCV

Published by Azul Editions
7804 Sycamore Drive
Falls Church, Virginia 22042
USA
azulpress@aol.com
Distributed by LPC Group/InBook:
1-800-243-0138

Front cover construction: "Sorrow" © Stasys Eldrigevicius

ISBN 1-885214-02-2
Cataloging in Publishing Number: 95-75219

Printed in the United States of America

First Edition
Second Printing

10 9 8 7 6 5 4 3 2

ACKNOWLEDGMENTS

Grateful acknowledgment is made to the editors of the following publications in which some of these poems appeared or are scheduled to appear:

A Celebration for Stanley Kunitz, Book of Birth, Confrontation, Contemporary Religious Poetry, European Judaism, Forward, Her Face in the Mirror, Jewish Identity Through Literature, Jerusalem Report, Journal of the American Medical Association, Lullwater Review, Passenger, Poetry, Poetry East, Ruby, Rage Before Pardon, Sifrut, Tikkun, The Plum Review, Trafika, Truth and Lamentation, Visions, Washington Writers' Publishing House Anthology, Without A Single Answer, Woman As Is: An Anthology of 20th Century Women's Poetry, WPFW Poetry Anthology.

Italicized passages on page 60 are taken from the *Book of Job.*

Part 8 of *Lithuania* is based in part on "Kalavrita of the Thousand Antigones" by Charlotte Delbo, from *Days and Memory* (Marlboro, Vermont: The Marlboro Press, 1990).

Lithuania (Parts 1-3) received the Anna Davidson Rosenberg Award in December 1993 from the Judah Magnes Museum.

CONTENTS

Poem Of The Mother

In Unfamiliar Air

For Betsy Buxer and Janice Eanet, dear sisters in life
And in memory of our Lithuanian family Volpe

PREFACE

The poem, *Lithuania,* is based upon the firsthand accounts of
elderly Lithuanians and surviving Lithuanian Jews, on letters
written from Lithuania to my family on the eve of World War
II, on diaries secretly kept, on conversations with a family mem-
ber who survived the Kovno Ghetto and Stutthof Concentra-
tion Camp, and on evidence still visible — massacre pits in every
town and village that I visited. It is based on the felt absence of
Jews in a place that had once been the center of world Jewry.

In 1944 the Kovno Ghetto was burned to the ground, leaving
crumbling masonry and chimneys. Of 30,000 Jews forced to live
in an area where previously 7,000 had lived, now only a small
number remained. Of those who had survived the years of star-
vation, illness, exposure to cold and forced labor, of those who
had not been killed or sent to concentration camps earlier, some
few escaped.

Of those remaining, some were murdered, some were removed
to concentration camps. Near the War's end, as the Russians
were approaching Danzig, the German guards of the Stutthof
Concentration Camp took their prisoners as hostages, loaded
them onto boats and embarked into the Baltic Sea. There they
were kept for eight days without food. In order to avoid having
the Allied soldiers discover the prisoners, the Germans pushed
them into the sea to drown. One of these — a member of my
family — was dragged out of the surf onto the beach at Kiel by a
British soldier. Only moments before rescue, her sister had
drowned.

Central killing places in Lithuania — the Ponar Forest outside of Vilnius, the IX Fort built by the Czars in Slobodka — were places of particular horror. If you go to Ponar today, you will see the massacre pits. You will see flowers that grow beside them drained of color, their ghostly stamens tipped in blood. You will come to a pit being excavated where Jews were forced to live in winter, their job — to dig up the bodies of the dead for burning, to hide the evidence of what was done here.

The poem attempts to penetrate beneath the pastoral beauty of these places as they appear today — places where local people come to pick mushrooms or to gather wild strawberries — and to peel back the layers of earth and time, to touch the places where our people once lived and, by so doing, to touch them.

As the five-decade silence comes to an end in the Baltics, there is little time to learn about what happened there. Lithuania is only just beginning to come to terms with its painful legacy. In 1993, a woman called out to me as I drove through her town. She entered the automobile and sat beside me. She wanted to tell me about a man who had crawled out of a massacre pit only to be turned in and killed. A year later, reading my face, she identified me as a family member of her childhood friend before the War. We have not yet finished our conversation.

This poem is part of an ongoing exploration to learn through the "archives of the feet," in Simon Schama's words, about the presence and the absence of those I have come from.

— *Myra Sklarew*

ON MURANOWSKA STREET

ON MURANOWSKA STREET

I have always loved particulars: the angels
bearing a martyr's palm, the way the hair
of the worshippers forms waves or
filaments, the flowers embroidered
on your sleeve. Even my sleep
contains them: the pointed teeth
of mice, a black camera aimed
at my grief. Yet when you ask for the truth
I summon words empty
as air as if I were guarding a sorrow,
encapsulating it that nothing
might come into its vicinity, letting it
ripen. Like the foot of this woman swollen
with callouses, bearing
bits of earth and tar, thorns, remnants
salvaged in it like the map
of the world, pebbles filled with carbon
when the earth was young, fern still
coiled in sandstone. Never mind that he draws
this foot to his lips and kisses the world
that lies embedded in it, or that beneath
the bellies rolling down to her knees
he sees only the loveliest bones hidden
there, caverns and wetlands he traverses
easily, moving from opening
to opening like a bird metabolizing at a rate
too high to measure. He does not hear
the rifle fire behind her nor the fleeting
sound of hooves. He does not see
twenty men standing on Muranowska
Street, their hands raised in the air.

APRIL 1943: BORSZCZOW

Only you   little collarbone   dared
to sing in death's courtyard: *the Jews know*
nothing   yet they walk
in the marketplace at noon   they are hauled
to the graveyard   they kneel down   say
goodbye to the whiteness of light   the dead
no longer care what they wear   the others
carelessly wearing their clothes Spinka   little collar
button   when I lie down on the earth
is it you I hear   still singing
to that scattered remnant   or were you buried
alive in their courtyard   for loving them

ROSARY

In braille you read the oval
shapes with your fingers   they rise
in the earth necklace   float
through red clay   Call
the blue beads
to your fingertips   They open
and climb toward you   tendrils
of pain   they glide their blue
bodies under the field   One grows
there   one of them   clinging
to his wood

INTERVAL

We know
it is only a matter of time
before the distance
collapses in on us,
before we feel
the fur of the world:

              a train
bearing its cargo
of hands
holding our ankles down
while we strain
with our necks
for air

or an innocent helicopter
calmly patrolling
the river, brother
to the ones that carry
the wounded
back from the north,
the sky filled up
with their insect shapes.

              The feet
of the hanged ones
swing over our heads like
brass censers
from their chains.
Our frightened god flies
like a bat

through his cave.
At dawn
a horn will sound;
we dance on
numbed by a music
no revolution has prepared
while out on the floor
of the desert hunger
offers its breast.

THEN

for Paul Celan

I think just because you are
coming I can write the poem
of the creation of the world I
can put the Seine in my river poem
the temple of the cobblestone
cobblestones of liberation
in my poem because you are
coming. I think I can put the prefect
of police in my poem harvest
of exile golden badges sutured
like leaves into the bodies
of children. But it is not
like a door opening this poem not
willing like a finger dipped
in the earth. River this Seine
why do the threadbare badges cover
the surface of water
like petals river who touches
every groping heart are you the one
who received the poet his armful
of crystals that night in April
before the last darkness
of winter was washed off river
the poet walked that night
letting off breathing opening
his death like a jar.

HOMAGE TO SIENA

Senius sheltered here from the wrath
of his uncle Romulus who was abandoned
in infancy and suckled by a she-wolf.

If I press my face
against a wedge
of light, if I open
a wafer of air, will you
not hunger for breath?
If the train you are
riding passes between
thin fascia of stone
slicing the day,
would I not read your
sudden dark? Remember
the girl eating her terra
cotta orange, how she
opened the fragments
letting the sweet
juices run out? How
she was turning the glass
pages of her book?
And the necktie
of the man, how it hung
over his left shoulder
like a tongue?
And the sleeping boy's
feet doing their crooked
dance in the aisle?
How you sought
a sliver of light

around the edges
of the sealed
compartment, how you
hungered for air?
And the tiny
burned dresses covered
with ashes with
ashes and soot rising
to the surface
while the little ones
were eating the white
earth so sweetly, terra
alba, eating in their
miniature chenille
rooms in their organdy
their taffeta rooms?

WHAT WE WANT FROM OUR ENEMIES

Not retribution but what they've used: a metal
map box, food rations, a scrap

of cloth, wood from a fire, the living
ember, even a trip wire

fine as a hair, thread to explosives — anything
still bearing a trace of the enemy's body.

The Vietnam vet in the dark theatre warns: *Don't
touch it!* — when the soldiers reach

for the container belonging to the Viet Cong.
Too late: they are blown

to bits. *We wanted to know who they were.*
When the daughter of a Holocaust survivor lived

for some days with the son of a Nazi, she asked,
putting her arm through his: *How*

can I hate this man? He is like me.

So we crawl back
along the ledge of death

to this incongruous place: we touch the Nazi sons
as though they could lead us to the lost lives

of our parents, as though by knowing
them, we could at last witness the pure agony

of our mothers and fathers that we might pull them in
from the waters of their drowning.

THE MESSIAH RECONSIDERED

1

How often
and in what detail
we have imagined you.

Like the fine blades
of grass, the attention
to each wing petal
of the angel da Vinci made.

This is the way
we have counted off
the years
of your absence.

Weren't we warned
how blindness
does not imply
darkness.

So your absence
is composed of valleys,
of fiery delegations.

2

Oh all the armies
of messiahs — we are hemmed
in by them: a Cretan,

later a Persian who claimed
to have found
the Ten Lost Tribes.

One nearly
took hold — born
on the anniversary of the exile
to Babylon.

Sabbatai Zevi
who descended the husks
to redeem scattered
sparks of divine light.

3

Not much is said
of Sarah the orphaned
survivor he married.

Perhaps she lived many years
like her namesake
and bore him a son
in her old age.

Her husband
the messiah
converted to Islam.

4

Some of us say:
He has come.
See he lives here
among us.

Others tell
of the rabbi who slept
without undressing
six of the seven nights
of the week
in order to be ready
to greet him.
On the seventh
he took off his clothes:
sabbath is holier
than redemption.

5

What riddle
do we with our few days
make of our messiah —
That there is
no body lighter
than water?
How could he have walked
on the surface
like these words walking
on stilts
across the white page?

That there could be
between us this absence —
the comforting
conjunction of grooved
entablature, creases
in a band that rounds
the beloved head.

That we are not immune
from dreaming of him
like the shepherds
who looked up.

That we must
come back each year into
the vicinity
of our longing, back
to the neighborhood of
the possible.

THE CRY

Though the river
was rising
the whole night,
I did not notice
caught as I was
on the thorns and brambles
which circled the banks
singing their hallelujahs,
lifting their glasses of wine.

There was no flood,
only the feet of the waters
running in the night streets,
only the hands of the waters
knocking on all the doors,
only the wind coming off
the surface of the water
like a skin.

LITHUANIA

LITHUANIA

1

At three-thirty in the morning in America
I have filled an enamel soup pot with cold water
from the sink and I am watering
the apple tree I planted a summer ago,
I am watering the false camelia tree I planted
in March, the crown-of-thorns cactus,
the plant with tiny blue flowers. I am trying
to remember something.

I am trying to remember something I couldn't
possibly know. I am trying,
as I was two days ago in Lithuania,
to move by feel, to know when I was close
to where they had been. At first
I just walked in the Jew's town
without anyone helping me, without anyone
telling me. I walked until I remembered.

But how could I? I had not been here
before. Who could show me
the way? Neither stones
nor saints nor royalty. Perhaps a man
who bit the throat of a Lithuanian
before they cut him into pieces. Perhaps
a tiny red poppy I picked from the trench
of the massacre of Keidan — they say the weeds grew

here twice as tall as anywhere else. How
beautiful it is in Lithuania. See how at Ponar they come
to fetch mushrooms. It was their land long ago. This
was not the only killing they have known. They pick
apples and plums in this season. They pick
cherries. At Ponar they dig for
mushrooms and carry them home
and cook them and eat them--the mycelium

four hundred years in the making nourished
by countless wars, by betrayals, by blood and
bone, by the tears of the dead, by hair and skin. Every
hill is suspect, every ravine, every tree. If you put
your foot down on the earth in Keidan or Datnuva or
Ponar, if you stop walking and read the shape
of the earth under your foot, you can feel the skull
or a bone of someone you knew, someone

you almost remembered. In Kovno a man keeps
the bones of his family from Ponar in a glass
jar on his bookshelf, bones and a bit of earth.
A man keeps a list of the killers. Sometimes
he sends them anonymous letters,
warning them their time has come. Sometimes
he goes further, confronting them directly. He has
nothing more to lose. At his age he endangers

only himself. At Ponar there is a ladder on wheels,
its two parts fold down to the ground. What
is this for? It was used to climb up to the top
of the mound of dead bodies in order to throw
more of the dead onto the pile,
to burn them, to hide the evidence of what
was done here. In Kovno a man keeps a list
of the righteous among the nations. Case by case he documents

acts of kindness and rescue, the names
of those who risked their own lives to save others. Ponar
is a forest, a beautiful forest. The Jews walked
here at night in the dark. Some say they lit candles
to help them see where they were going. Others
say it was fear that showed them the way.
Dante was comforting: in his catalogue
of descents, cause and effect still reigned.

Even he took pity upon Paolo
and Francesca — lovers he treated so tenderly.
But here there was no reason
apart from designation. I name you, tree,
for death. I name you, star, for death, you
grass, you earth, you sister, father. I
name you Christ, I name you Jew name you.
In the territory of the forbidden

like the green ailanthus which dares to grow
in the interstices of stone, they found
what home they could. They occupied air.

2

As in the days of my father's death when I did
not want to be called back from the opening
through which he was leaving me,
lest I lose sight of him, that if
I turned back to the world, he would be gone
from me forever, I ask my life for silence, for
time, that I may see only the images of Lithuania.
I am trying to remember something. At Passover,

though my Lithuanian grandfather died before I was born,
I always remember him standing
at the head of the table. Strange,
because at Passover we eat reclining.
When the plane hovered over the airfield
in Lithuania just before landing, it looked
like a museum of the ancient wars — helicopters
with wooden propellers like windmills,

World War I airplanes. A strange assortment
of leftovers from various occupations. *Gorbachov!*
explained a man two rows
back. On that first day I walked for miles.
Then I took a tram but couldn't figure
out how to pay. The driver, his body
inserted between glass shields, shrugged
and I shrugged and got off. These are peripheral

notes. I am trying to remember something.
But I stay out of the center
of memory as though it would explode
in my hands if I touched it. I wanted to go there
by feel, to see if Lithuania would tell me
its secrets, to see if I would
recognize myself in Lithuania, to marry the myth
of who I am with the myth of place. To find more

than the signs of the dead. To find evidence
of the lives of those I have come from. Or to give up
Lithuania once and for all. On the airfield
as we landed something was moving
across my field of vision — an old man in a wooden
cart pulled by a horse
as if one century moved through the axis
of another. Like the wooden house of the last

century wedged between two stone ones. Perhaps
one of my family lived in this house.
How to tell this — like a gospel to say
four versions. Or to say what
is left out. Or to frame the city as the
stage for the drama of salvation,
parables flocking to it
like birds of the air. There is no way

to make the journey to this place. We circle
it, we read it like a map of a district, we name
its alleyways and its houses. We draw in closer
like the camera's eye but we describe
shadows, we describe air fence
lattice petrol cudgel wooden club
water hose gully blood we describe
a man, hardly more than a boy.

He leans on a wooden club, resting —
his murdered lie at his feet his dying
at his feet, his club thick as an arm
high as his chest, he is wearing
a fine suit of clothing his hair
is combed. A group of Jewish men guarded
by armed civilians wait their turn. Within forty-five
minutes the young man has beaten

them to death. And when he is done,
he puts his club to one side
and climbs on the corpses and plays
the Lithuanian national anthem
on his accordion to the clapping
and singing of the nearby civilians —
women hold up their small children to see.
At Keidan in order to cover the cries

of the Jews forced to strip at the mouth
of a mass grave, the Lithuanians started up their tractor
motors. Those not killed by machine guns were buried
alive. All this was watched by the principal
of the high school, the mayor, and a young
priest. Afterwards, the Lithuanians told that when
the pit was covered with a bit of earth, the surface
heaved up and down as if a live pulse

emanated from that mass grave. In order to stop
the heaving of the blood earth, the Lithuanians
used rollers to press the earth down. The names
of the towns of my family were called Kovno, Volpa,
Keidan, Datnuva, Rasein, Siauliai, Jonava, Pilsiu, Krok.
1939: *Dear Aunt Sara Rivka: Don't be anxious.*
With us things are as they were. We hear about the war
but we don't see it. Russia has just given Vilna

to Lithuania. It is a poor region. We don't know
what will be. We hope for the best. I remember a woman
who sat on the pot where the apples cooked in the cold
basement, her face black from smoke. And here, near this brick
building with a red tile roof, is one of our family, Mausa
Volpe, hatmaker. And nearby, his cousin Aaron. And
here live two killers of Keidan. When I talk to them,
I make them afraid. And here is the hill

where two sisters ran up and down in order
to lose weight. But they fell ill. And
this is the place where I accidentally killed a kitten — it was
caught in the door. We held a funeral
near the River Nevezis in Keidan. And this is the shop
where Jewish property — after the massacre — was sold
very cheap, three marks for a big bag. The buyer
took his bag to his waiting cart, anxious

to see what he had got: the bag was full of tfillin —
phylacteries used by religious Jews
for prayer. The man didn't know
what these were. Furious, he rode up on the bridge
over the river and threw the tfillin into the water, the dark straps
spreading out like hair in the river.
Here in America, if you rise early enough, in the dark,
if you go out of doors, you can smell autumn

though it is still August. Here and there leaves are beginning
to fall, a few under the dogwood tree, oak leaves, poplar. And just after
dusk, when the earth passes through the dust stream of old comets, if
you look up you will see
meteor showers, the Perseids. Are these burning songs
striking at our atmosphere like the hearts
of those who met their deaths untimely in Lithuania?
I tell you, once we have found our dead, though we cannot hear their

answering voices among the sounds of this world, we will tear
open the skin of the earth
to admit them. We will not lose them again.

3

But is this the way their story will end?
Not this way. Not yet.
For here is the place where the young brother
was killed, his wife, the infant nearly ready
to enter this world. In the fire that burned
the mother alive, the baby exploded from her
belly like the sacred letters of the scroll
Akiba was wrapped in when the Romans

set him afire. Wedged between the life
before life and the life to come, for a single
moment the child looked upon this world
before it too entered the flames. An old woman —
her face so close I hear her labored
breathing, I smell her skin — thinks we are
survivors come back, pierces the silence with a voice
so calamitous, tells us about her neighbor

who escaped from the pit in Krakiai
where all others were murdered. He went
to the people to whom he had entrusted his
property, but they betrayed him, sending
him back to his death. Is she one of the righteous
or one who is haunted by the past? Or one
who fears the survivor who will turn up
one day at her door and ask for his house

back, ask for a place to breathe again, ask
what has become of his small son?
They cut off the head of the rabbi
of this town and set it in the window. Was he
to be a talisman, keeping watch over
them like a ship's figurehead sighting
the dangers before them? Or an object
of ridicule? Or by fixing his head

like a beacon light in their window, they could hold
imprisoned the heart of his people? What hatred, what
fear carries human action to this place?

4

This then is the story of my people, the story of what
became of my family--those who had not come away
earlier, those who survived the pogroms
after the assassination of Czar Alexander II. At Keidan
after the massacre of 2000 Jews
one escaped who afterwards hid in the forest
in a bunker. Through the night and in early
morning kind villagers brought him food.

The head of the village discovered some coming
with food and offered 10,000 marks' reward for the man
dead or alive. He invited the police. Twenty of them
circled the bunker dug into the earth, a small chimney
for fresh air. They issued an ultimatum to come out
or they would set off explosives deep in the earth.
The man, half asleep, thinking he was already dead,
arose, wearing one shoe and carrying two grenades.

Pretending to surrender, he attempted to explode
the first grenade but had forgotten to put off
the ring. He fell back to the earth, repeating the episode
with the grenade, this time exploding it. Some were
killed, some wounded. Till they got their consciousness
back, he escaped. He came to the house of
villagers. What happened after, what I want
to tell — they put him on the oven, he had fallen sick

from the cold and the snow and suddenly he saw
on the peasants' hut parchment of the Torah glued
to the walls. He knew them to be good people but
he was frightened and escaped from the oven: "I must
go," he insisted. Later he came back, he found
the Torah had been cut from the walls and replaced
with newspapers. Those who lived in the house
had understood why he had run away from them.

After the War, he considered the day of his escape
from the bunker as his second birth
and on that day each year he fasted.
Here is the house of Yankele Gross — Pasmilga 2.
We would close the windows on Easter
when they came from St. George's Church.
They would start to drink. You never knew
what would happen. And here is the house

where the wife spent all their money
on shopping. But it was not allowed for a Jew
to go hungry on the Sabbath. All the families
would raise funds for food. And here
is the house with the thatched roof. When the
goat got hungry we would take straw
from the roof. And here is where the chief
of the firemen lived, Zodek, who dared

to resist the murders and was brutally killed.
And here Rifka, beautiful but meshugah. In winter,
normal; in summer she would go naked
through the streets. And here the Bet Midrash
with the big arch on top and the sundial with Hebrew
letters: Yud Aleph, Yud Bet. And here we
joke with the women who have come
out to the fence to talk with us: Perhaps we

will take back your house. Startled, they laugh. And here
is the cheder lived in by a peasant and soon
to be destroyed. And here a long wooden
house where Moshe Leib Lilienblum was
born. It was also a tea house. You had to bring
your own sugar. In the bottom of this house
I was born, a man tells me. What was it like
getting born in this house? I don't remember.

But I know for certain I was born naked.
The youngest of eight children. Two weeks later my father
died of tuberculosis. And my mother lost her milk. I was nursed
by a wet nurse. I have a milk brother in Israel.
And here we used to eat mice. The purpose of a piece
of bread was to catch a mouse. Now one of the mouse eaters
is a pilot in the Israeli air force. Not poor, not rich, not drunk-
ards — earth, a cow, a few cucumbers. One brother twenty-one

years old was as a father for me. All to the left
of Smilgos Street was the Ghetto. The Smilga River:
old Jewish cemetery on one shore; mass grave on the other.

5

In Vilnius, outside my window, three boys throw
broken glass bottles at one another. Now the glass
shatters against the building, now it showers down
on the victim. Sometimes the thrower trips
on the garbage or debris of building materials. One
is the target; the others the shooters. Then the game
changes: everyone for himself. At first I peer
from a corner of the window. Then I stand framed

in the window so they can see me. The sounds
of broken glass, their high-pitched shouts
cease. At Ponar, while they dug up the bodies
for burning, a few of the Jews dug a tunnel from the pit that
they might escape into the forest. But along
its entire route, the tunnel had been mined. My mother
loved the small pears just come into season,
like those on the table of the old ones in Datnuva.

My Lithuanian grandmother preserved cherries,
removing the stones with a hairpin and a cork. On
the table in Datnuva are quart jars of cherries. Chaya
brings me a bag of small pears to take to America
but I leave them for one who will come here
after me. In Lithuania we are under the ozone hole,
fearful of the sun. A man tells me, Here, a big hole was dug.
They were looking for gold, gold teeth, gold

wedding rings, rummaging among the bones
of the dead. Ten years ago I found a black scalp
with hair. I was sure it was my father's brother.
After the killing this was a bald field. They grew up
by themselves, these trees. We understood
because here these weeds were higher, twice,
than the others. August 28, 1941: The local
collaborators under the SS killed two thousand and

seventy-six people. The local chief doctor
supervised the process. The first group
of one hundred people — elderly, the sick — brought
here, alive. Among them, my mother. Zodek
saw the first group ordered to take off their clothing.
Two men refused. Zodek grabbed a pistol from the hand
of the killer, shot him in the back. The doctor
couldn't help the killer. Two hours later he

died in the hospital. On the third day, his funeral.
One thousand people came. On his tombstone,
it was written: This man died through his duty.
Zodek threw into the pit one German commandant,
jumped with him into the pit and was hit with a pistol,
his teeth in his throat. The other Lithuanian jumped
into the pit. He used a knife to cut Zodek and saved
the commandant. And one more incident: One Jew

had hidden a knife and he beat one collaborator
he knew who was brought
to the hospital. He told the doctor he wanted
to participate in the Jewish killing and came back.
After the War the death sentence was banned.
The murderer was sentenced to 15 years.
He spent 12 years in prison; later he lived near Datnuva
until his natural death. Vacationing

school pupils used to participate in the killings. The doctor was
brought to trial not because of his experiences in the War
but as a thief, sentenced to five years.

6

Be wary of old forts — they have a history
of killing; their walls are used to the screams
of prisoners, the silence of death. Their walls
are impervious to the last messages
scrawled in blood. There is no poetry in any
of this. These forts have witnessed
the deaths of over 100,000 Jews. Be wary
of names. Those who took the long

road from ordinary life to the ghetto and
from the ghetto to the Ninth Fort called that way
Via Dolorosa — Christ's walk
to Golgotha. The road that led uphill from
Kovno to the Ninth Fort. The Germans called it
the Way to Heaven — *Der Weg*
zur Himmel-Fahrt. And in secret they named it
Place of Extermination No 2, *Vernichtungstelle nr.2.*

Not existing place, *vernichtungstelle.* No,
that's not quite it. A transitive word, more active —
place to make nothing, to nullify, cancel, annul.
You must say these names yourself. Taste
the strange mixtures of annihilation, the Jew
using Christian iconography, going in columns
of a hundred along the sorrowful way.
In the Ninth Fort the power went off. We

stood in the cold dark, in the cold, in the
dark. We could smell the air they had breathed.
I wanted, above all, to escape. But I kept
my feet on the ground. We lighted candles
and we walked through the steel blackness.
The woman with me had worked there twelve years.
Her face had no expression as she talked about what
happened there, the voice drilling into my head.

In the barracks, dug deep into the ground, heavy
steel doors. Deep trenches surrounding the
fortifications. High concrete walls, rows of barbed
wire. Trucks whose motors were run to drown
out the sound of crying, of shooting. Guards
who beat and chased them into the path of the guns
of the Lithuanian partisans. *October 4: Kovno, 9th fort —*
315 Jewish men, 712 Jewish women,

818 Jewish children (punitive action because
a German policeman was shot at in the ghetto). October 29:
Kovno, 9th fort — 2,007 Jewish men, 2,920 Jewish women,
4,273 Jewish children (removal from the ghetto of surplus Jews).
Digging and burning. What was
buried had to be unburied. The Master of Fire,
the expert on burning supervised the firemen,
three hundred bodies exhumed and burned

each day until the flour of dead souls disappeared
in the earth or fled upward into the air.

7

In the cemetery at Keidan the stones
are covered with moss and earth. You pick
leaves, a handful of stems and broad leaves
wide across as your two hands
and you scrub the surface
of stone clean. You take leaves
from the moist earth and kneel
down and make an opening in the moss

and earth until the carved letters speak again.
Like a bright face, the names are whole, we say
them aloud. Sometimes at night,
if I take the magnifying glass and enter the forest
of Ponar or climb above the River Obelis,
walk in the newly formed woods, a few grave stones left
for the resting dead, if I put my face close
to the photograph, it seems I can enter

there with my body. That I am there.
Now I look closely at their faces, those
who guard the entrance to the town of Datnuva
where once my family grew flax and made linen,
they guard their cache of pears, apples, cucumbers,
cabbage, cherries. I want to ask . . .
oh at night how I long to ask them
to tell me about my family if I promise

not to judge them. At night I clear
a space around this as if I were
going on a long journey and must leave
things in good order,
in readiness for someone else.
I want the center to open. Nothing
to interfere. The way at night I open
the package and take out the pictures

and with a magnifying glass
enter the green world inside,
as though my body has physically
moved into their spaces, as though
I am once again in Lithuania.
In this courtyard where once the living
dreamed as you dream: touch
this leaf, that strong trunk.

Touch the petals of the poppy
as they did. Perhaps someone has left you
a message, a strip of bark torn away
by a finger, now high over you
in that birch. Go on, go down.
Go further on. A child said: I want to be
a dog. A child said: I hid here.
A child said: I could not hide here.

A woman in Girkalnis, for
offering food and water to the Jews,
was locked up with them
in the cloister of her church
without water or food until some
went mad. Until they were taken
to a pit and massacred, the little ones
hung by their feet and broken

against trees. At Ponar
there are flowers that grow
over the mass graves, ghost
flowers, mutants with nature's colors
wrung out of them, their white
stamens tipped in blood.
The harvest holiday was kept
in October. It was celebrated

in the forest and all in the village took
part, bringing the dark bread, beer. Animals
were sacrificed to the gods. The souls
of the dead were invited home
and provided spare chairs and towels.
Tables were filled with food and drink
for the returning souls.
After the souls were cared for, the villagers

bathed themselves in the river.
They called the liquidation
of the Jews *Erntefest* — harvest festival.
Later, when it was done,
and the land which rested in the confluence
of two great rivers was covered
with water, the inhabitants
grew fearful and went to the cemetery

and took off the Jews' clothing.
They threw the belongings of the dead Jews
over the fence into the cemetery in order to make
the flood waters recede. In Slobodka,
the headless body of the chief rabbi was found
still seated near an open volume of the Talmud
he had been studying. In those days

it was said that if you removed
the head of a people, then it was not difficult
to destroy the body.

8

What I remember is not how they were
rounded up like animals, caught
like fish in a net, beaten and shouted at, dragged
over the fallen bodies of their kind, not how
they stood against a wall or at the edge
of a ravine or a pit or a trench they themselves
were forced to dig, knowing
it was for their own graves, not how they were

bludgeoned or blasted out of this life,
nor what they thought or felt as they breathed
in the air of their last moments, but
what happened afterward. The single human
acts that came afterwards. We know about the killings,
we have seen the pictures, read the descriptions, heard
the testimonies. We know nothing about the killings.
How could we? But what happened afterward.

How the women who were not burned
alive in the school house or the church or their villages
sent the smallest children home and walked up
to the edge of the ravine to see
for themselves. How they stepped carefully
among the bodies until they found their own: brothers, sons,
fathers. How they tenderly held their hands,
their heads, still warm. How they did not know

what to do. How they removed the wedding rings
from the fingers before they grew stiff and wore,
from that day on, two rings on their wedding finger.
How that night they came with candles
and kept a vigil so their dear ones would not
be alone all night. How in the morning they came with water
and cloths and washed their dead and prepared them
for burial. How they carried each of them on a palette

to the graveyard, 1300 of them. How the other villagers
came to help them. And they set them in the center
of the cemetery and with the stones of the stony fields
they built a wall around them, to keep them from wild
animals, to give them the burial every dead one deserves.
But for mine, the tender acts afterward were not
possible, not the hands on their faces, nor the white
cloths to wash them, nor a few drops of water,

nor their faces turned upward to the opening
sky, but thrown down, eyes wide against the blood earth,
in whatever state they happened to fall, whatever moment
of surprise or pain. Nor were there any to find them, to carry
them, to console my dead. Afterward, to cover their actions,
those barely alive were forced to dig up the bodies out of the
pits, the ravines, to prepare a place for burning, a stack of logs,
a row of bodies, logs, bodies, orderly but for the power of the

odor of death, but for the decay of death, the fires taking them,
taking the living, not even washing
the dead, not even burying our dead, not even, not

9

When Joseph caught sight of his
brothers tending their father's flock
in Dothan, he approached eagerly. *Behold,*
they said, seeing their young brother
in the distance: *Here comes our little dreamer.*
They conspired to slay the boy, to throw
him into a pit. Later they will say
to their father: *An animal has devoured*

your son Joseph. A father is pointing
to the sky. He is stroking the boy's head.
An old woman is singing to the baby
in her arms. The SS guard at the pit shouts
something to his comrade. We cannot hear
what he says. The family climbs down into the pit,
lines up against the dead. For those who cannot
walk, others already naked carry the fragile

bodies of the still living into the pit. Here in America
a child asks — Why is there an earthquake?
Is it because God wants to punish
the earth? — all the while moving her head
first to one side, then to the other like the periscope
of a submarine, feeling the air with her head.
As she speaks another temblor
passes through the earth.

In Keidan, the earth of the trench where the murdered were
buried seems to pull away from the surrounding earth as if the
sacred burial place could not bear to touch the adjacent soil.

What is the nature of the pit which has been made?
With what instruments was it dug? Or with whose bare
hands? And what was encountered in the earth
when the digging commenced? Who prepared
the pit? And did they stand back to back,
or in rows? Did they work in stages or in shifts?
And who commanded the digging. Was there one pit
or many? Did the people walk of their own accord

from the barricaded trains to the pit
or were they beaten and whipped as they were driven
off the trains? Were they dead or alive
when they entered the pit? Were the pits dug
by the Russians for the storage of oil?
Or by the Lithuanians for the bodies of Jews?
Or by the Jews? When the Jews were sent
from Kovno to Slobodka — 30,000 to fit

into the space for 7,000 — the Germans
required 50 the first day and 100 the next
to build the barbed wire fence--first
the ghetto, then a concentration camp
which would be their route to death.
A man remembers a Russian song: "Bricklayer,
bricklayer, for whom do you lay these bricks?
We have no time to tell you. We are busy

building a prison for ourselves."
What are the true dimensions of a pit?
How deep is a pit which must hold
50,000 people? Shall they be murdered facing up
or facing down? How shall their clothes
be sorted afterward? Or shall they be required
to place their clothing in the correct
piles beforehand: shoes in one pile,

underclothes in another, outer
clothing in a third. At Ponar some went down alive
into the pit, a fine covering of earth
closed about them. And they perished.
And some went down alive and no covering
of earth came to them. And some
who were devoured in the earth were brought up
to the light once more to be set

ablaze in the light of burning. Of these
there was found a mother holding the hand
of her child. *My days are past,
my purposes broken off . . . if I look for the nether-world
as my house, if I have spread my couch
in the darkness, if I have said to corruption: Thou
art my father, to the worm: Thou art my mother
and my sister, Where then is my hope.*

*He hath fenced up my way that I cannot pass.
He hath broken me down on every side and
I am gone and my hope hath He plucked up like a tree.*

LOOKING AT MEN

LOOKING AT MEN

Yesterday, a man asked me why I was
traveling alone. If he were my husband, he
would not permit me to go away. It says
in the Koran the woman is the comfort of
the man's body.   *   The men took
turns picking leeches off each other's
bodies. When the war ended, the smell
of fresh soap made them vomit.   *   A
man and his son and a horse. The father
says: Get up on the horse. As they
journey they pass a jeering crowd. How
can you let your old father walk while you
ride? they ask the boy. The father
climbs up behind the son and they
continue on their journey. They pass a
group of people working in a field. How
can you both ride, wearing out your old
horse? they ask. In the end the father
and son carry the horse.   *   I watch a
man quicken as he crosses a mine field,
as he climbs into a bunker and takes up
his sub-machine gun.   *   Replacements
have come for instruction. The sergeant
picks up a smooth metal ring. Do you
know, he looks into their boys' faces,
what these can do?   *   Beneath me a
man's head is the only marker as he
walks the labyrinth of trenches; this one's
never seen war. He feels the earth
around his body, the closest he's come
to his own grave.   *   At night a man

smokes a cigarette when he cannot
sleep. These are true stories of a
personal nature. * From letters I know
how a man wishes to be seen. From
sleeping with him I know how a man is.
  * Under me a man holds perfectly
still to see how long he can stay inside
me without coming. * A man, partly
blind, touches my back lightly with one
finger to learn where he is in this world.
I mistake it for love. * Lady, a man calls
to me, beautiful lady, if only you knew
what you wanted, I would show it to you.

TWENTY-FOUR HOURS

I had twenty-four
hours
to erase
from your body
the crust
of this world.

Chaval, Pity, you said
and we unwrapped
each other

like unlacing
the threads
which bind together
the pages of a book,

our hands touching
and going away again

like touching a town
on the map
in the morning
and then being there
at nightfall.

TRANSPLANT

They used to bring
a bit of soil
from the old country
to the new.

Or at burial
a handful
of sand
from the desert
to accompany
the dead
on the long journey
from diaspora
to resurrection.

Or now
without soil
or sand
seed
from the inner courtyard
dispersed
between the legs
of the exiled.

IN BED

Jewish extremities — cold
hands and cold feet,
all that long history
stretching back before Christ
and the Magi
or going forth into who knows what
calamity.

Why do you have such cold hands?
he wants to know.

It's the history, I say to him
while he blows on my fingers,
while he prevents me from wrapping cold
around his body.
The history blowing through these rooms,
I tell him. The old story of exile
and assassination.

Why are your toes so cold? he asks
cradling my feet in his own.

The history, I reiterate, warming
to this dialectic. The way the history
goes from one desert to another. Or stalls,
I think to myself, in some cozy doctrine
certain as the yellow-backed antelope
bedded down in straw, the afternoon sun
encircling her.

BORDER DISPUTE

My neighbor puts a survey
stake in the middle
of my yard; I put a stick
with a white flag
in his: surrender. He plants
a yew tree next to his
wooden survey marker, its red
plastic ribbon flowing
over my land. I put an otter
in his yard. In the otter's mouth
I place a white flag. Surrender.
My neighbor builds a red
fence between my land
and his. I put a white flag
on top of his fence.
In my neighbor's
bathtub coming up
between his legs is a wooden
marker. On the end, a red
ribbon. I tie a white string
around the red ribbon.
Surrender. In my neighbor's
bed is a wooden woman. Between
her teeth, a red plastic
ribbon. Mine, says the ribbon.
Mine. Mine. I tie a white
ribbon to the end of the red.
My neighbor builds a small
boat in the creek bed which
marks the boundary between his
land and mine. All day

he sails down and up the earthen
rift singing Mine, Mine,
the red plastic ribbons
streaming like northern lights
from his oars.

DEADLY NIGHTSHADE

You bring me green
leaves from the mountain, the cool
night still in them. *Vlita!*
you tell me. I scramble

to look up the word
in my green dictionary. You throw
the book out of the window.
I see the words drift

off the thin pages, falling here
and there in the mountain.
You put your body squarely
before me: *Vlita!*

Stryknos! Ah, strychnine: a central
nervous system poison. From deadly
nightshade. But I prefer
death to a loss of honor.

In the interest
of survival, I hesitate.
Later, you come to check on me.
The *Vlita?* you ask.

Soon, I say, putting you off.
Go home, I plead with you.
When I can see your back leaning
at right angles to the

mountain, your hands clenched
behind you, the measured
pace, I boil the poisonous
leaves. I pour off the first water,

boil them a second time.
When all of this is done, I take up
my green poison, as good a place
as any to get my last view

of this world. I use lemon
and oil. I taste your mountain.
All evening I wait. And then
you return. Odysseus looming

in my doorway, no old nurse to
recognize you, not even a dog
sniffing out his master.
Only this woman with her great

cooking vessels. You carry each one
to the marble sink. You pour out
the dark waters and shake your head,
cold distance between us expanding

like the universe until our laughter
rises to the cypress beams
overhead and returns, warming
our small chamber of light.

KNOWING

1

When did the light go
out of the stone? Permanent
knowledge slip off
leaving behind a few words
on a page, the only thin clue
to its nature?

2

I know when I stand
on a mountain terrace, my two arms
reaching up into olive
branches, gray-green leaves
narrow as cilia recording
the wind, ripe olives letting
go down an invisible
channel to the sack
at my feet, I hear my body
sing my body sang
as I reached through the branches
to touch an old man's hand.

3

It didn't happen that way: the old man
was sick and stayed behind
in the village and though

I was not
welcome I went
anyway down the ancient
stone path to the slope
below. Vangelis
cursed when he heard me
coming and climbed higher
into the tree his ladder
like Jacob's barely
touching the earth
as though he would enter
the sky to escape
this paroush, this
stranger.

4

Once I wore this totem
world. My ancestors moved
easily between its skin
and mine. Now all my dead
are enemies. I take
as my bed the catacomb
of the thornbush.
And under my head.

5

If these words are reliques
of another age, breathe them in
whose root is ritual.
It was ours once.

Didn't you know the gods
are at home
in the mountains.
They too witness the birth
of the unanswering sky.

6

I came forth that day despite
Vangelis. I reached
my arms into his tree, tore
at the branches, black olives
and green — whatever
was left — and the olives took
on a life of their own they
rolled down that mountain
toward the black sea
purple and green olives
trembled as a wall of water
curled over them and took
them out into the deep.

7

And what could any man
say then? Not even
the ministrations of the wind
that day nor Cristina kneeling
on the earth could cancel
fear. Not the white cloths
bound on her head as if she had
stepped forth from an ancient

tableau; no surrender in the round
metal pans filled with goat's milk
nor the acorns she scooped
from among animal droppings.

8

And later, when Vangelis left
his saddle on my porch
to tell me that in his eyes
I was already far
from that place, I touched
the wood carved by a man's hand
rubbed by his body. I touch
the goat skin and the woven
blanket sewn beneath it.
I touch the cord looped around
the wooden crosspieces. I put my two
hands on his saddle old as Homer
so heavy I cannot lift it
and when I touch Vangelis'
saddle I also touch him
and he knows it.

FORGETTING

How sweet is the landscape
of forgetting: no
trembling arrow
soaring from the past —
the present
forming beneath our fingertips.

Let the past be severed
like the head
of a chicken, only the dumb
clucking of that head going off
in the barnyard like a fizzled
canister
and the clumsy body propped
on its scaly legs,
improbable corpus scattering
to the four winds.

Let all judgment be
made of the bones
of the moment.

Witness us like the man
who steps off into the future.
Or pity us carping at his side
like those who stood on either
side of a savior —
the shadow of the past strangled
in the trees.

SACRIFICE

It is said
that for a man
the earth
is his mother.

But in Jerusalem
they say
that a man
takes the earth
as his wife.

That these fruits
of that earth — grape,
spikenard, cluster
of henna and green fig —
these are his offspring.

Remnants
brought to the table
innocent of the meal
as Isaac on his mountain,
as the ram of Abraham
at Moriah.

DINAH

And Dinah the daughter of Leah, whom she had borne unto Jacob,
went out to see the daughters of the land. And Shechem
the son of Hamor the Hivite, the prince of the land, saw her;
and he took her, and lay with her, and humbled her.
Genesis 34: 1-2

Dinah

I tried to tell my brothers I loved
the man. That I went out
of my own accord
like Noah's raven
to test the landscape of the new.
But Simeon and Levi could not
hear me. Later, people whispered:
Like mother, like daughter.

Simeon and Levi

We are safe. No one in future will tell
of this lowing herd, undermined
like the wall of Jericho the wall
of Shechem — on the third day its sinews
severed, its strength brought
down. No word of this son of Hamor
reckless as water
who humbled our sister Dinah.

Dinah

At first I struggled under him.
Then I heard the scraping
of an angel's brittle wings trapped
in the world. I felt the shudder
of those answering wings
on their forlorn hinges. Can you feel
the presence of the angel spread
over us like the sky? I asked him.

Shechem, Son of Hamor

I see light where it crawls
along the ground. I see
pelicans who fly through water,
water which sits
on the surface of air.
Let no angel confuse us
with blindness that we weary
of finding the door.

Dinah

After my brothers
brought me out from the house
of Shechem, my name fell
among the ashes.
Was she fair? they asked.
And did she bear young?

Was she numbered among those
who went down to Egypt?
Or did my father Jacob
invent me, that in the land
of calamities they could stop
their wandering, even in this place
where the Kingdom of Israel
broke into twelve pieces.

Jacob's Silence

You asked why I did
not stop them, my sons Simeon and Levi,
when, on the third day, after the men
of Shechem were circumcized,
they took their revenge.
Or why I permitted the girl
to go out to the daughters
of the land, why that, in the first place.

Dinah

But tell me: what has become
of the promise of descendants
and land? From Sinai to here
we floated in the bedrock
of time; we made
of the moment our clay
and our earth. We made
our homeland in a wedge of years.

Shechem

Do you know the story
of the man who needed a tongue?
You do not need this tongue, he told
me, and he took mine. And I could
not speak. He needed a leg
to walk on, so he took mine.
And an arm to carry his child. He
borrowed mine.

And when he was done, when he
had taken everything
he looked at me: Now walk, he said.
Such is the nature
of promises.

Dinah

Here, in this place where Abraham
built an altar, where the Assyrians
destroyed Shechem, here
where the body of Joseph
was carried from Egypt
and buried in my father's plot,

like Isaac's silence after Abraham
returned from Moriah,
they have not told us
how it went later
in these fertile lands under the shadow
of the mount of blessings
nor in the scorched earth
beneath the mount of curses.

LOD MASSACRE

You have pasted up
green trees
in the right-hand corner
of this gray envelope
of land.

You have sent in
prophets who are recruits
and after them
the dust
to dry up their words.

I ask you —
are these not reunions?
Even this stain of blood
which lies down
with the stone.

AT THE SYRIAN BORDER

Walking between two mine fields
I pretend I am a tourist here: What trees,
I say. What mountains. I mouth
slogans bitter as a salt sea.

The wind feeds on the basalt rock.
Under every eucalyptus there is
the yawning shadow of a bunker. My people
is an armed camp.

I remember a boy who made a bridge
of his body for the others to climb across.
They turned him into air and fire and earth.
And here is the place where a father

let his child down a knotted sheet
like Jacob, only not going up.
One child by one child down the ladder
of knots and when he himself climbed

down for the last time he found each one
murdered. O Jacob let us put away
our strange gods. My people is an armed
camp. Her sons wear old faces.

WATER

Though I am thirsty I do not drink
water nor cup water in my palms
nor pour water
over my head and face nor put my feet
in water. Though I am made
of water and I require it,
though soon water will fall
down onto the earth and drain
slowly away through the sandy pores,
though finches
will sip water from the beaks
of their parents, I withhold
water and do not drink. Though water is
everywhere in this glacier-swept land,
ridges and inclines carved
into ponds into lakes and rivers,
though the light comes
through an opening in the roof
of the world in ways it hasn't before,
causing there to be more
water, still I do not partake of it.
Yesterday as I crossed a field
at midday, the sound of heat nearly sent
me reeling though I never let on
that I was losing my way
so the man beside me would not
think me soft or less capable.
I thought about that quality of light,
the terrifying and unrelieved
light coupled
with the burning heat of that midday
and I did not temper it with water.

THE GOODBYE

This endsaying — moon pried loose
by grave force, pulled
out of earth's sweet atmosphere —
this has been formulated in every place.
In each text it is known.

At birth, the broken covenant
with before — parting from it hand
over hand along the dark way,
or valve closing
on its nine month work — breath
in the place of blood.

Or in sleep — it rises
like a ghostly glacier
bounded on each side
by consciousness;
it calls us
and we go at night
to that kindly absence —
sealed ark
bearing us toward morning.

Or in the sudden heat of love
when the body senses the cold deeply
like breathing in.
The Goodbye — it is well known.
What more to say of it?

We play it back — old film,
refugees in our torn ships, sailing

the bruised distance.

We walk upright on this earth
for our allotted time. Love,
we pass you as before. Yet
this passing has the shape
of farewell.

CERTAINTY

I have begun to forget the meaning of words. Arieh writes
to me from his settlement in the south to say that the
khamsin has come early. Does it come before summer?
Before spring? *Autumn*: dusk? *Autumn*. I have lost it. Its
certainty. The way it once had an irrevocable meaning, its
definition contained in it like a nucleus. It wears that
definition loosely now, like a hat which blows off in the
slightest wind.

Arieh is coming home.It is better to write of a thing before
it happens. Afterward one must deal with the facts. But
before, one can imagine the whole event, add to it,
embellish it. Before, the events stretch out in all their
possible forms. She wakes up, goes to the door and finds
him waiting there. Or, she has just prepared the meal. And he
comes in then. She takes his coat and sets him down to
the table and serves him the cabbage and eggplant and
tomatoes she has grown herself. The rosemary pointing
up the flavor, the spokes of the herb like signals in the
sauce.

Signals of warning? *Autumn*. The word has a buzz at the
end that is felt at the back of the throat. The mouth opens
on it and closes like the shell of a clam. Fall. In the
northern hemisphere. In the southern hemisphere, that
time from the March equinox to the June solstice. You
see, each idea seemed perfectly clear once. Each word.
Without conditions, without exceptions. Does the water in
the tub drain out clockwise or counterclockwise? Which
hemisphere is this, actually?

*In the zone of the doldrums the wind has almost stopped
altogether. Horses harnessed to the equator can no
longer pull the earth in its orbit, so affected are they by
the intense heat.*

He writes that there are troop movements to the east. That
they have had to rise early for two weeks to go on
maneuvers. That the sudden activity has him worried.
They cannot clear their heads during this time of the hot
winds. They are irritable. He writes that there is a peculiar
expectancy, the way a certain sound at a high frequency
enters your consciousness and you suddenly become
aware that your whole attention is fastened to it, that you
have begun to wait for that moment when it will cease.
Like pain.

It is not his custom to warn me of his arrivals. He likes a
certain tension, a suspense about his comings and
goings. I have grown to like that as well. And anyhow, it
is a reminder that certainty is something we want, not a
quality of this world, not of this life. For hasn't the old
woman died without asking if we minded. Netka, how was
it you didn't wait for me to come home, to come to your
side that night? But just died, quietly, alone. And Chanah,
after the weeks, a whole year at your side, you waited till
I had gone home to my own bed to sleep before you
relinquished this life. I arrived there that morning to find
your face raised to the light, your mouth in a peaceful
smile as though you had discovered something we
weren't ever to know, as if you had gone over to a place
we hadn't any business in. And anyway, what would I
have done had I been there at that moment of leaving?
Would it have been different?

Death. There's another one. Hearth, breath. Wreathe. *Death*. If I say it often enough, the word shakes off its meaning like the dust of the rug Semmel beats in his window, like the dress Yenne shakes, the slight shudder of her body inside. Only the thick feel of my tongue between my teeth when I come down on the final consonants, the muffling of sound like the cover of snow, like the blanket that covered Chanah's face that morning, when two strangers came to take her from the room.

At Eilat there is a hot wind that comes from Africa. When you breathe it in, your nostrils burn. Your bare arms feel hot to the touch. Though you are out of doors, between desert and sea, breathing itself brings a sense of claustrophobia.

The conversation begins as though it has never ended. As though he hadn't left. The odor of other places is on him. I try to decipher the geography of his passage. I make a map and I place him here, here. All the while he talks. I wonder if he has slept in the beds of other women. I wonder what they look like. He talks. I do not listen. Sometimes a word falls onto my plate. I pick it up idly on my fork and taste it. It is salty on the tip of my tongue. Another word. Sometimes bitter at the edges. At first I do not listen. It takes me a long while to gather up what was once between us, to take the words I have sent to others and call them in. Like a shepherd calling his flock at evening. I call them home so they can be his again.

I lay in the bed with my legs in the position of running. He on his side with his two arms in sleep out in front of him as though he were waiting to receive something. I imagine

I am running down the stairs, turning off a light, washing clothes, cooking a meal. My thoughts race. Toward morning I turn to him, my breasts touch his back. I listen for the sound of his breathing which has become regular and deep. I try to imagine his dream. He turns toward me and I place my body between his outstretched arms.

IN THE TRAIL OF THE SLUG

It's a patient trail, scrolling
off the stone walk
in a curve. I try to imagine
what the slug thought: *Enough*
on this grayblue step, the cold
pouring into my moist belly.
Let me bury my face in green.
And once down on the earth it spreads
its skirts, its beveled edges
the way the manta rays ripple their lovely
edges, their protein wings through
the sea. Or like the delicate clitoris
as it rises like sea grass from between
the labia, probing the golden
air. Like that. There is something sexual
about the nakedness of the slug.
Its skin missing. Like our clothes
fallen away beyond us. Or the way we have lost
our boundaries and driven into one another
beyond all that separates us.
Like that. That something so vulnerable, so
open could survive in the world.

ESCAPE

When you looked up
I was gone,
my sadness small enough
it could fit
into the palm of my left
hand, no place
to come back to
at night.
After that
I traveled freely,
my image cancelled
in the others.
I was light then
like a nation newly conceived
where they are still trying
to make up
its constitution.
In me
they have not yet found
declarations,
statutes, nor covenant.

POEM OF THE MOTHER

POEM OF THE MOTHER

The heart goes out ahead
scouting for him
while I stay at home
keeping the fire,
holding the house down
around myself
like a skirt from the high wind.

The boy does not know
how my eye strains to make out
his small animal shape
swimming hard across the future
nor that I have strengthened myself
like the wood side of this house
for his benefit.

I stay still
so he can rail against me.
I stay at the fixed center of things
like a jar on its shelf
or the clock on the mantel
so when his time comes
he can leave me.

A PLACE

We have come to a place
where language ends, the words
short-circuit on the page.
Which word can contain a boy
broken into or a girl laid down
on the packed earth of a schoolyard
in September, her body taking
the fists of a boy screaming Jew Jew.
This is not a poem of sorrow
or complaint.
Not a poem to find out
why a child
in a lonely basement
offered her breasts to us.

AT YEHUDA'S WEDDING

At Yehuda's wedding
the children
hold the canopy up.

In our lives
the children come
to hold us up

over their heads
like cloth and glass.

They wear us
like a tallit.
We are knotted
and fringed.

We have come
from the four corners
of the earth.

And under their feet
our hearts
like the wine glass
the bridegroom
crushes with his strong
heel.

BECOMING A JEW

When I was born
they called me a Jew.
I hurried to put on
the shoes
of a Jew. I hurried
to put on the hat
of a Jew. But still
I wasn't a Jew.
In the mirror I tried
to read the difference
between us. But my red
hair, my pale skin
refused to explain it.
They asked if I
believed in their God.
I put a star
on a chain at my neck
but like the dress
of my sister
it did not fit.
They gave my sister
a cloth badge
and she sewed it on
with perfect stitches,
with fine black thread.
They took my sister
away to the center
of our city and left
her there without food
or water. For seven days.
We did not see

my sister again.
The young boys began
sailing their bodies
through the glass
windows like kites.
My father's tears
on the stone step.
My father's name.

CROSSING OVER

When my first child tore
loose from me
the old woman cautioned: Bite off
her nails with your teeth
and bury them in the earth.

In the fall of that year
the feet of Abraham
went overhead — Isaac his son
at his side, the wood
for the burnt offering sprouting
leaves at one end, root hairs
at the other.
And the fire
in the father's hands
sent up its bright alphabet,
a signal to Sarah.
In the narrow passage between intent
and act,
the angel's call
and the confusion of the ram.

Here, on our side
in the Feast of Booths
the trees
have put out too much fruit
as though after the long drought
they might not survive: black walnuts,
acorns not yet ripe, tough capsules
propelled through the air
without letup;

the knobs leave their imprint
on the soles of our feet.

In the firmament
between worlds the guardian
of invalid prayers — those uttered
with the lips, the heart
dragging behind — urges us
to delay awhile.

What doors must close
before this one can open?
And which angel
rises up through the brickwork
of sapphire
to bid farewell
to this child torn out
of the distance
like the leaf of the ash I tear off
to find
in back of each green shape
a seed
trawling in the morning light.

DREAMING OF RAIN

1

Nothing is left
but the tracks of the water
and the sound
the rain made as it withdrew
from sleep's house
like a tidal wave that turns
on its heel and departs
leaving the floor of the sea
suddenly naked.

2

It was a good, a drenching
rain. I knelt on the earth
just before it began and took up
a sample in my hands: quartz
and mica shone on my fingers,
the spent earth fell
back among the seed coats.
How is it the wild
strawberry finds sustenance
here? The notched petals
of the dogwood are drawn tight
as though someone pulled
on a thread.

3

You touch the dust
under your shoes and ask: Am I
made of this?
And the water
answers.

4

Many nights the rain visited
like that, opening itself
to the earth, its sac of waters
prelude to the rebirth.
And we stood
helplessly by in our doorways
sending our fingers
like Pharoah's daughter out
into the river
to claim what the water
had washed down to us.

5

I see by a cloud that has slipped
into the earth
the rain has been here during the night.
But we had no sign of it while we slept,
only the seed coats falling
silently to the roof.

6

When the water came, pitched
like stones, we did not stop
dreaming of it;
we fell asleep eagerly
taking the dust of the dry earth
with us into the deepest room.

THE MISSING

When you take a word
out of a poem — say *world*
or *wind* or *mistake* — the place
where it was can't seem
to fill up. Like taking
a boy out of the world, however
he might have chosen it.
So when we say the names
of the living, the boy seems
to be standing here too, holding
his name. In the painting
I was working on last
night, a pregnant woman
is looking out at the
trees, but it is the dark
goblet on the table I ask
you to notice, the way
what I've painted out
forms a shadow so deep, it
overwhelms the woman, the trees.
Once in August our ship could
not approach the island
called Hydra, the seas were
rough. Now Hydra is part
of what little baggage
I carry with me. All
that has been erased
is inside us, singing. Word.
Or boy. Goblet. My double-
headed hydra, how you proliferate,
all your eyes looking up
through the vivid
network of the missing.

WHEN THE YOUNG DIE

When the young die, do they leave
behind their eyes? Are these their days

not yet lived? Have they taken
away with them the delicate flower

of our safety? And this floating wound
in us — is it their deaths

that refuse to heal? Or like a rib erased
and another written in, is it

their absence we feel in the place
of bone? Are these their nights coiled

and not opening, like instructions folded
into the template of the gene? When the young

die they pull at us like an ocean
pulling at the shore. Is it they

who pull at us now
like the mouths of newborns

at the nipple so hard our bodies
give way suddenly like sand.

IN UNFAMILIAR AIR

SAPPHO'S MOTHER

Nineteen years
since she has seen me,

since a small crescent moon
curve of orange she couldn't

swallow
lay pressed against the inside

of her cheek.
Would she say — *I measure*

my absence by
all you discovered

and abandoned,

by the sharp outlines
of your sorrow like stones

on the hungry beach.
Or like all mothers — *Can't you do something*

with your hair? How cold it is. Why don't
you cover your head?

Stop scribbling. Come to the table.
Time for supper.

TOGETHER

When I was done
with the bursting part — rupture,
intestinal contents spewed out,
colon silent as stone, done
with the damage
the body was trying to heal
but couldn't, when I was
done with the helping
part, the cutting open part,
the part where the wound
was daily debrided, gauze pulling
dead tissue away from living, leaving
the long wound, blood, granulation
tissue trying to close a place
that belonged to me and
didn't, a place I observed
with a curious interest, then my life
took over saying *I have left too much*
in your hands. It's my turn
now. It was my life that turned me out
of my bed and sent me walking
on stork legs, my head
uncertain above me
in a wilderness of air.
Trust me, my life
seemed to be saying. And took hold
of me and didn't let go this
time. And we walked together, slowly
at first, in those strange streets
of recovery and the body's loss.

TINNITUS

It is always with me
now, a nimbus
of sound like
a crown of white noise.
Fenestra, mark
of the moth's false eye. Os,
opening. Membrane.
Ear's drum. Sound.

Like witnessing
the knife's edge
as it is drawn
down along the surface
of skin just as you go
under, wings climbing
beyond consciousness.

Air waves lapping
against the ear
drum like the sea. Lost
for years in the labyrinth
of images, I attend now
as whales do to the silence
between sounds.
I am never alone.

Silence filled
with a sound my body
made before the world
was taken from me, muffled
and lost like fluid

that rises in the carpenter's
level, tilting the earth
away from me.

If the earth could not hear . . .
if instead it was given
this white noise covering
the fields in thin ash,
given a pulse which sounds
over the fields
like grief, this immortal
residue like a swarm of

bees sending out the body's
signals when the
bones have gone to dust.

LEARNING TO LEAD

You try to teach me, I try
to learn — consolidation
of power, who is boss, lock
the door. I listen
to you. I try to pay
attention (What is the name
of that red bird? Whose hand
touched me last
night?). Oh Boris, may
the wind shake a few
leaves from our tree. Come
lead us, your roofer told you.
If you are truly Boris
Pasternak. A little vodka.
Sausage. A few roots holding
us to the earth. Can't anyone
remember I am the middle
of seven daughters? Every day
I start out like a knight
on his quest, like James
who stands here in my doorway,
a latter-day Van Gogh, the wind
drifting among the pages
of his long red beard. I say
to James: You are our knight.
He loads his wheelbarrow with bunches
of watercress he's picked at dawn
from a secret cache by the spring
house. You've found the grail,
I tell him. He looks at me strangely,
goes out through the doorway. But now

he turns back quite suddenly: "We do
our best," the red wisps
of hair and the straw hat the last
I see of him for awhile. Oh Boris
and James and me: Today
is the first day of trout
season. No matter how,
a new morning has come and we
are firmly resolved to lead.
No matter. Here comes
the little wind again. I hear
a few leaves falling. See
how we are all
falling onto the ground.

NELL'S STORY

Oh I opened my eyes, my eyes all right and it was light
greeted me, light rising up and I went to see what could
be causing it. And it was fire causing it. My scream went
out of me without asking permission, oh my scream
tumbled out of me until even I couldn't tell where it was
coming from. The others slept in a room off the kitchen.
I screamed and ran out of the house in my bare feet — it was
20 below — and ran round to the back of the house and
tapped on their window. The husband got up and broke
the glass. I could see the wife moving in the room. She
came near the window carrying the infant in her arms but
when I looked next there was no infant, only the shoulders
of the wife coming toward me through the window. I
pulled on her arms and her shoulders to fit her out
through the broken glass and the smoke came billowing
out behind her but there was no baby, no baby in her
arms. And the thud I heard: Was it the husband going
down to the floor or the baby she dropped as she came
through the window? And what did the wife think when
she got out in the snow and the sound what sound did
the baby make and what did the husband say eating his
dinner of smoke and flames? What did my feet say
running in the snow? And what did the dogs say when I
fell among them, running to safety and fallen on the
ground, the dogs scrambling over me while I propped
myself up on the hind quarters of one of them and rose
up tall and went on running? And what did my feet say all
those months, poor feet who didn't belong to their shoes?
Oh my feet who didn't belong to their shoes. And the
baby who fell with a thud on the floor. And the husband
eating his supper, oh his supper of fire and smoke.

SONG OF THE LOST DAYS

So I wasted some days.
Some I held
like bright blue
eggs between thumb
and forefinger
not letting them
break. Or breaking
them open, hurricane
of yolk. Or asking
them to sing,
my fingers touching
their throats.
Some I used well:
they were filled
with four kinds of
weather, with wave upon
wave, like the
generations.
Others — I asked
too much of them.
How could they contain
cities of fire, covenant,
altar or memory?
In this chronicle
of vanished
time, lost days, do you
wait for me at the end
of the street?
Or have you gone out
early, before
the seven
suns rise above the field?

PRECISION

This could be a day like that —
all you dreamed of
coming to pass. The mountains being
one size. Someone who
asks for you. No one ever leaving.
Is that what you want? Not exactly.

Then what? Something about the sadness
when the light comes back again.
Something about the mornings
where you drift out of reach
of anyone. Or the tin nights stapled
to your chest like a message.

That? Not exactly. Then what?
The names of your dead gathered up
from the forgetful dust. Your beliefs
painted on the missing trees. All the archways
weary of the distance coming in
closer. The earth, bending to listen.

TOWARD EVENING

Toward evening I begin
to miss the earth   its small shudder
as it turns in its cradle
of liquid air   the odor

of matted fibers decaying   the outlines
of leaves saying   *I am the name*
of your harvest   spores sending up
their everlasting notes   I open

the door of my house and call
the earth back   First the roiling
molten core comes hesitantly   then
the mantle glides over it

like a shoe to its foot   then stones
back into the riverbed   water
and the firmament of water   You know
the story

When I have assembled the earth
I step out into its offerings   I kneel
in the rain touching
the tawny surface

the gills of mushrooms   the way
you might reach out idly
to touch an animal who knows you
my fingers trace

the patches of universal veils   gemlike
crusts deadly
and   beautiful   torn ring and sheathing
cup of the destroying

angel   I don't want to be
afraid of what grows here   not of these
bright shapes burrowing
into air nor what the body offers

IF THE DEAD RETURN TO US

If the dead return to us,
they will come in
to our wounded houses as if
they know the way.
They will carry a flock of stone
birds the dark seeds
of winter still
in their beaks, their jagged
flight.
      If you come
on the third night of the war
you will bring the song
of your last day on earth, you will wear
your pain carefully so we do not
recognize it for what it is.
The others will ask: Has he returned?
Has he come to live
among us again?
      If you come into my house,
I will open my body to you, I will touch
you the way one snow
crystal falls
to another, I will touch
you carefully so as not to hurt
you anymore. And we will be
together like the husband and wife
in the old woman's painting: the sky
is blue, there are lakes
and mountains. Only here can the two
meet again.
      I don't know what
happens next — if she tells him

she stood in the dark
places like the dead or if
she moves her hands
over his body, closing
her eyes that she might read him before
she is chased off
by the wind,
       before she forgets
this topography. I don't know
if this is the place
where he says: I have always
loved you. Or if he could not bear
even the weight of her fingers.
Or if in the morning
like the moon
she could no longer find
him in the white sky.

SELF-PORTRAIT AS VIGIL

for Gregory Gillespie

You only appear
to have staved off
the danger, your shaved head
trapped in green space, torso
barely able to rise
from the east. Behind you
blue backs off. Not even
a sky. Beware this devouring
monotony, the way the past
inhabits it or lies
in wait at the end
of a street or threatens
to cry out from the folds
in your sheet
or to appear suddenly
like a peat body washed
to the surface. Beware: blood
buried among root hairs will not
stay put. It will rise up
along the sieve plates
and thrust itself like limb
buds from the unyielding
branch into leaf. And when
you press the delicate fur
of a new leaf against
your face, like the broken
stem of blood root,
it will stain your skin,
it will cry out.

GREEK EASTER

Kristos Anesti. He is risen.
One priest for seven villages, how
our Babas flies to arrive
before the sun. And the other one
is driven in his wooden
cart at midnight round and round
the village church. How tenderly
they carry him, as though
they have found in him the green
sea. How they brought him up on
the mountain, nails and thorn,
sought his help among the dusty
stones, that he might look up
from his casket into the feathery
sky of their evening and bless
them. As if the small ones
kneeling beneath the stained
robes of the Babas could sense
his presence. As if they could
rise along the liquid skirts
of the priest up into the vineyards
above their village, that
this once they might go beyond
themselves before they are sent back
to the nearby air of their ordinary
lives, kneeling once more — *Kyriaki* —
on a Sunday at the feet
of their priest, tiny harbingers
remembering only that once
they were roused and saw rivers
opening on the high hills.

WHEN IT WAS SPRING

After the winter we let the earth
in as far as the gate as far
as the eyelid's edge where a tear
mingled with light. We let
the wheeltrack of the earth
come round to the steps of the house
where my seven brothers kept watch over
the injured last-born. Our enemy stretched
over us a line of confusion,
saying to the boy: Lie down
Lie down on the earth. We thought surely
he would take our young brother's
life. The boy lay
himself down on the earth believing
he would not rise up any more.
And our enemy opened his pack. He took
out clean bandages, gauze
and alcohol and tended his small enemy's
wounds. And the earth with its wheeltracks
and its abstract light of these days
bore in its arms the sudden
warning call of the dove, bore
a turtle as wide across as a man's
arm, this earth came bearing the ways
we devise to bring sorrow
to one another like a grain-offering.

IN UNFAMILIAR AIR

1

Prisoner, how will you leave
empty these rooms, battalions of ice
and weather, places
you were stored for the duration
like goods?

Like this stillborn packed
in his earthen crypt
to wait out the season. Or a bird
rooted in yolk,
timing gone awry: its flight
folded in like the fingers
of your hands just beginning to touch
air.

2

True, you still look
around yourself to see if someone
is following, someone taking
notes. And then you begin
to believe you can walk down any street.
Equal parts past and future, after

and before. Is sorrow
your season? Must we live in it
as if it were ours? As if sorrow could tell us
something we needed to know? Or can we

shunt it like a vessel, its lumen
obstructed, so it will not
pass this way again?

3

Prisoner, tell us how
once you have lived
in this place you can love
the world again. Any more than this child —
her face severed at the crown and drawn

down like the slip
of a woman bunched at her ankles —
will not bear
in the circuitry of delicate tissues
exposed under the surgeon's
tools the story of loss. Or a barrier
broken.

4

Leaving or staying: what to do
with this life and its untellable transitions.
Who do you talk to, prisoner, sitting
at night on your lonely
hill, silence building up slowly

out of which anything can take form?
That time rides in you
like a parcel of light
moving toward us from a dark age.

O neighbor, do not lift
you fine head
toward us. Simply live. Live in your durable
house while we quarrel at the threshold.

AFTER THE EARTHQUAKE

1

A woman reports her bed
is shaking, animals
stream through the walls.

No one believes her.

She reports when she strays
into the world, her feet
are swallowed up in a black
squall of water.

The others want proof.

She reports on the end
of longing: east
inside the skin
or west, the separated

halves in platonic embrace.

2

A woman reports how
the gods of the three
great religions play

bocci on the temple
mount while police

locked in a booth

are set afire,
the prayers
of the righteous

leashed in like rage.

3

But was there
an earthquake?

Or smoke
in the throat of
its victim
making confession?

Or rain
driven by a refusal
to collaborate?

4

The dismantling
of the wall — did we look
as if on a forbidden

act, our hands
the only witnesses
to the mortar clots
departing the prohibited

space?

Did we cross over

feeling the resistance
of air trapped
in that stony chamber
for years?

        5

Should we have listened
to the woman's report?

Even the gods looked
up from their game.

What can the blue
innocence of the sky

this morning tell us?
Or the nasturtium leaf harnessed
by a single thread

its crimson
trumpet unafflicted,
a luminous

secretion buried
somewhere in its heart
trying

to forecast a season.

REFUSAL

In August
you died
and in September
the year
turned around
regardless
In October
the leaves
on signal
depart
their trees
On signal
the flies
grow sluggish
in the window
well
Frost crystals
line up
on the glass
Only I
am recalcitrant
refusing
to put away
the leather band
that circled
your wrist
clockhouse
with its contents
fallen
out of time

MAP

I made a map from the parts
of your life and I carry it around
like an idiot child.

It clings to my side, pointing
dumbly at the world. Poor scholar,
it has forgotten so much:

who goes before Abraham and which
brother killed which, who dressed
in the skin of a goat.

I tell my map to make a line
through all points above sea level;
I tell it blue for oceans, green

for lowlands. But it only shows
which territories were lost
and which sons.

My map doesn't know how many years
between this night and the one
where we said goodbye.

There are so many things I wanted
to ask you, so many things
I have tried to tell you.

ODE TO THE CZAR'S ASSASSIN

1

*I sing of the Czar's
assassin, of his knife,*

*of the delicate thread
he winds three times*

*around the neck
of Czar Alexander the Second.*

*I sing to the words he whispers
as he helps Alexander*

*take his last breath.
It is to him I owe my life.*

2

*I thank the Czar's assassin
for scaring my little grandmother,*

*for sending her flying with her feather
bed and a few metal pots*

*and pans into the new world.
I sing to Czar Alexander's*

mother who foolishly
entrusted her child to the poet

Vasily Zhukovsky who wrapped him
in verses and trained him

to be gentle. Alas, see how poetry
can ruin a man!

3

I sing to Alexander
who took the silver tracks

that carried his people from Moscow
to Petersburg and stretched

them across the world, rail lines opening
outward like his freed people.

That is how he let my little
grandmother begin to dream.

4

I sing to the Czar's assassin
for reminding her

to be afraid. I sing
to my grandmother's fear,

to her snail's antennae
that sniffed the dangerous

air of Lithuania, to her mother
who packed a wicker

basket so full
three strong men had to carry it.

I sing to the useless
items she dragged from the old world

to the new, to the embroidered bedsheets
hairpins, to the delicate cups

and saucers that would break
along the way, to the feathers

plucked one
by one that would gather beads

of moisture and sink
to the bottom of the wicker basket.

5

I sing to my grandmother's
high-buttoned shoes.

I sing to her old legs years later
when I knelt before her

and pulled at the layers
of rubber stockings like bark

on a tree. I sing
to the child whose fear

took her away from the oak trees,
the beloved language

the rivers and fields
of her life.

6

I praise the Czar's assassin
who kept me from being bones

in the graveyard, blood earth
in the massacre pit

provender for the sacred oaks.
I would have been birch

or flax, rye seed in their bread, spore
in their mushroom, wild

strawberry, filament
of hair, cry for help scratched

into the wall of the Czar's fortress
or cell in the great wash

of their Nieman their Neris — twin
rivers pulling at the shore.

7

I sing to the Czar's assassin
for not letting

my grandmother feel at home
in Lithuania.

For giving me my life, so I could, one day,
return to the rivers, the stones,

to the earth of her childhood
that reaching across

the landscape of my mother's body
I could walk in my grandmother's steps.

ABOUT THE POET

MYRA SKLAREW's award winning work consists of seven books of poetry and one book of short fiction, including her most recent collection, *Eating the White Earth* (Tag press, 1994) and *From the Backyard of the Diaspora*, which won the National Jewish Book Council Award for Poetry and the Di Castagnola Award. She is currently professor of Literature at The American University in Washington, D.C.